Great Fire & Plague

ST

ST

The
Great Plague

Deborah Fox

Heinemann
LIBRARY

www.heinemann.co.uk/library
Visit our website to find out more information about Heinemann Library books.

To order:

 Phone 44 (0) 1865 888066

 Send a fax to 44 (0) 1865 314091

 Visit the Heinemann Bookshop at www.heinemann.co.uk/library to browse our catalogue
and order online.

First published in Great Britain by Heinemann Library, Halley Court, Jordan Hill, Oxford OX2 8EJ, a division of Reed Educational and Professional Publishing Ltd. Heinemann is a registered trademark of Reed Educational & Professional Publishing Ltd.

OXFORD MELBOURNE AUCKLAND JOHANNESBURG BLANTYRE
GABORONE IBADAN PORTSMOUTH (NH) USA CHICAGO

Designed by Joanna Hinton-Malivoire
Illustrations by Peter Bull Art Studio
Originated by Repro Multi Warna
Printed by South China Printing Company, Hong Kong/China

ISBN 0 431 12332 2   (hardback)
06 05 04 03 02
10 9 8 7 6 5 4 3 2 1

ISBN 0 431 12338 1
06 05 04 03 02
10 9 8 7 6 5 4 3 2 1

British Library Cataloguing in Publication Data
Fox, Deborah
    How do we know about the Great Plague?
    1. Plague - England - London - History - 17th Century - Juvenile literature
    2. London (England) - History - 17th Century - Juvenile literature
    I. Title II. The Great Plague
    942.1'066

Acknowledgements
The Publishers would like to thank the following for permission to reproduce photographs: Bridgeman Art Library: p21; John Walmsley: p4; Magdalene College, Cambridge: p24; Mansell Collection: p22; Mary Evans Picture Library: p25; Museum of London: p26; Wellcome Library: pp20, 27.

Cover photograph reproduced with permission of Mary Evans Picture Library.

Every effort has been made to contact copyright holders of any material reproduced in this book. Any omissions will be rectified in subsequent printings if notice is given to the Publisher.

Words printed in **bold letters like these** are explained in the Glossary

Contents

Ring o' roses

This book tells you the story of a terrible disease, called the plague, that killed thousands of people a long time ago, and how we know that it happened.

'Ring-a-ring o' roses,
A pocket full of posies,
Tish-oo, Tish-oo,
We all fall down.'

Have you ever sung this rhyme? It is about an event that happened in 1665. The **victims** sneezed a lot, so in the rhyme, 'Tish-oo' stands for sneezing. 'We all fall down' meant that they finally died.

Signs of illness

In Autumn 1664 some people living in London started to feel very ill. Strange dark lumps appeared on their bodies. They felt cold and shivery and then hot and very sick.

The doctors who came to their houses were baffled by the **symptoms**. They were not sure what to do.

Lord have mercy upon us

By Spring 1665, more and more people were ill. The news spread that the plague had come back. The last serious plague was in 1625 when over 40,000 people had died.

People with the plague had to stay at home for 40 days until they got better or died. Guards stood at the door to stop anyone leaving. A red cross on the door warned people to stay away.

Panic

Some people believed that if they built bonfires in the streets, the flames would clean the air. Others thought that dogs and cats were spreading the disease, so many of them were killed.

But the real reason for the plague was
rats. The rats lived among the rubbish
that people threw into the streets.
Fleas bit the rats and then bit
humans, which spread the disease.

Fleeing London

King Charles II escaped from London in June and many other people fled too. Doctors and nurses hurried away. Plague victims went to **pest-houses** when they had nowhere else to go.

But the people who left London were often **shunned** when they arrived in other towns and villages. People were frightened of catching the plague.

Bring out your dead

It was a very hot summer in 1665. By July over 1000 people were dying every week. By the end of September the number was about 6500 per week. **Gravediggers** had to dig more graves.

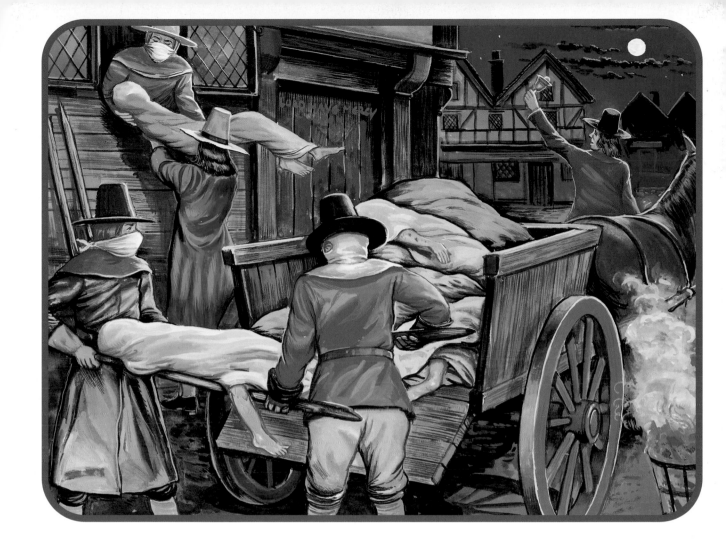

In the middle of the night the **body collectors** drove their carts through the streets, crying out, 'Bring out your dead. Bring out your dead.'

People return

When the graveyards were full,
gravediggers dug huge pits and
tipped the bodies into them.

By November the plague was disappearing and by December very few people were dying. People felt it was safe to return to London. The King came back on 1 February 1666.

The plague and other cities

People in other towns still did not want to **trade** with London though. They were frightened that anything arriving from the city would bring the plague.

The plague took many months to die out completely, and some people believe the Great Fire of London helped. The bad news was that it spread to other places in England.

How do we know?

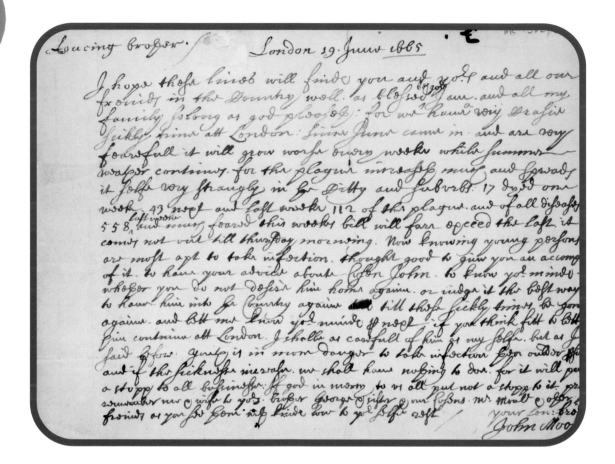

This letter was written in June 1665 by a London merchant called John Moore. It describes the first stages of the Great Plague. It is now in a London museum.

Daniel Defoe is a famous author who was a young boy when the plague hit London. Years later he wrote a book called *A Journal of the Plague Year.*

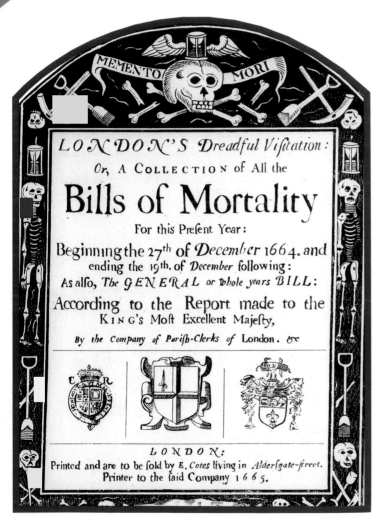

LONDON'S Dreadful Vifitation:

Or, A COLLECTION of All the

Bills of Mortality

For this Prefent Year:

Beginning the 27th of December 1664. and ending the 19th. of December following: As alfo, The GENERAL or whole years BILL:

According to the Report made to the KING's Moft Excellent Majefty,

By the Company of Parifh-Clerks of London. &c

LONDON:

Printed and are to be fold by E. Cotes living in Alderfgate-ftreet. Printer to the faid Company 1665.

At the time of the plague, the local **parish** kept a record of all deaths they knew about. They were called the 'Bills of Mortality'. The Bills showed how many people died and why. In 1665 the Bills said that 97,147 people had died. In 1664 only 18,297 people had died.

The Great Plague of 1665 was written about at St Bartholomew's Hospital in London. On 2 September 1665 the hospital records say:

"this howsie is visited"

This sentence means that the plague had come to the hospital.

The records show too that many frightened doctors left the hospital and London. The staff who stayed received some money as a reward for being brave.

Thomas Gray, surgeon £30

*Francis Bernard, **apothecary** £25*

Fifteen nurses £37 8 shillings and 6 pence

Drawings

Burying the dead with a bell before them.

This drawing shows the body of a plague victim being carried through Covent Garden in London.

Here you can see the plague victims being tipped into graves at night.

Objects and clothes

The buriers of the dead rung a bell to warn people that they were carrying the bodies of plague victims. This bell is now in the Museum of London.

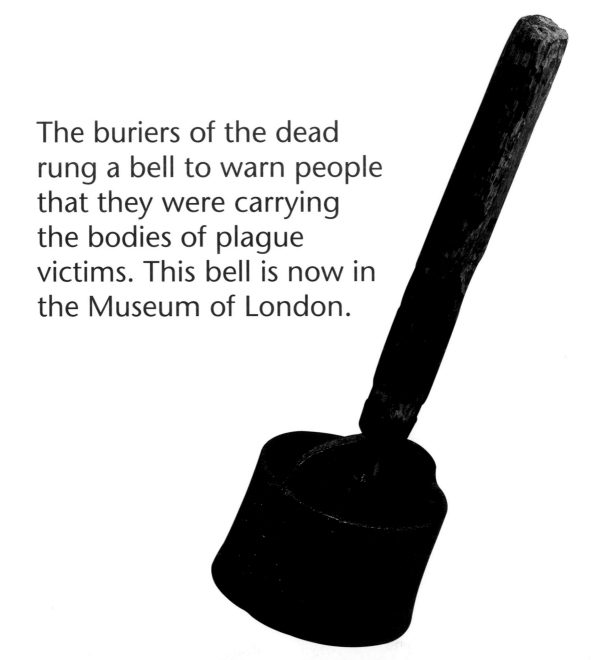

Doctors wore clothes like these to protect them from catching the plague.

Timeline

Late Autumn 1664 The first **symptoms** of the Great Plague appear.

April 1665 More people have the symptoms of the plague.

June 1665 Other areas of London get the plague. King Charles II leaves London.

July 1665 Over 1000 people a week die from the disease.

Mid-July 1665 The Lord Mayor orders that dogs and cats should be killed.

September 1665 Over 26,000 people die.

December 1665 The plague has practically disappeared.

1 February 1666 The King returns to London. It is estimated that between 80,000 to 100,000 people have died from the plague out of a total population of about 460,000.

1666 About 2000 deaths from the plague are recorded in London for the year. It spreads to other parts of the country.

1667 The plague disappears.

Biographies

King Charles II

King Charles II was born in 1630. He became King of England in May 1660 when he was 30 years old. In 1663 Holland suffered an attack of the Plague. Charles stopped trading with the country to try and prevent the Plague reaching England. This didn't work and the plague hit in 1665. Charles escaped to Oxford in June and did not feel it was safe to return until February 1666. Charles continued to rule England until he died in 1685.

Daniel Defoe

Daniel Defoe was only five years old when the plague broke out. His father sold tallow, which candles are made from. The family stayed in London during the Great Plague. His most famous novel, *Robinson Crusoe*, was published in 1719. He wrote *A Journal of the Plague Year* in 1722. Defoe died in 1731.

Glossary

apothecary someone who made up and then sold medicine to people who were ill

body collectors people who collected dead bodies

gravediggers people who dug graves

parish towns were divided into areas, or parishes. Each parish had its own church and it kept lists of all the people who were born, lived and died in that parish.

pest-houses hospitals for treating people with diseases

shunned avoided; kept away from

symptoms changes that happen to someone's body which show that the person has a disease

tapestry a heavy piece of material that often hangs on a wall. On it is a picture or pattern that has been woven with threads or wool.

trade to buy and sell things

victim a person who is harmed by something or someone

Further reading

How do we know about…? The Great Fire,
Deborah Fox, Heinemann Library, 2002

You may need help to read this book:
Turning Points in History: Great Plague and Fire,
Richard Tames, Heinemann Library, 1998

Index

Titles in the *How do we know about ...?* series include:

Hardback   0 431 12333 0

Hardback   0 431 12331 4

Hardback   0 431 12332 2

Hardback   0 431 12330 6

Find out about the other titles in this series on our website www.heinemann.co.uk/library